Promises in the Dust

Promises
in
the Dust

Bill Bauer

B k M k P R E S S

THE UNIVERSITY OF MISSOURI-KANSAS CITY

Many people supported me in the publication of these poems. I especially thank two poets, Dan Jaffe and David Anstaett, for taking the time from their own poems to hold me accountable for the lines in mine, and two early life mentors, Robert Lakas, S.J., who fought hard for a modern day renaissance in the American city, and Donald D."Casey" Jones of the *Kansas City Star* who, among other things, taught me how to cook eggs sherry, how to be a gentleman, and about oriental art.

My deep appreciation to Rae Furnish and Vicky Terry, who dedicated their time and caring to the actual production of the book.

Cover photograph by Chuck Goldschmid (Vietnam 1968), boy on roadside, trying to sell frozen bananas.

Design production by Michael Annis/Publication Services.

LIBRARY OF CONGRESS CATALOGING - IN - PUBLICATION DATA

Bauer, Bill, 1944 -
    Promises in the dust : poetry / by Bill Bauer.
        p.   cm.
    ISBN 1-886157-01-4
    I. Title.
PS3552.A83563C48   1995
811'.54--dc20   94-43704
                                                                CIP

 Financial assistance for this book has been provided by the Missouri Arts Council, a state agency.

BkMk PRESS
of the University of Missouri-Kansas City

Dan Jaffe, Director

In gratitude to those who reached out to a sometimes
raw and unruly boy of the streets, I offer this book to the
children of the world who have been abandoned or betrayed.

PROMISES IN THE DUST

Children Of The Dust   /   9

Initiation   /   11

Leather Jackets   /   12

American Dachau   /   13

Balls   /   14

Discovering The Solar System   /   15

Lion Tamers   /   16

Buddy   /   17

On Plato   /   19

Two Young Gays Watching Old Movies   /   21

Children Of Pan   /   22

The Pigeons Of Chernoble   /   23

Snapping Beans, 1955   /   25

Hornets   /   27

Dry River   /   28

Cottonmouths   /   29

Western Kansas Girl   /   30

Buffalo Mountain   /   31

Tequa Creek   /   32

A Lion In Kansas   /   33

Horse On A Hill   /   34

The Young Husband   /   35

The Farmer's Widow At His Grave / 36

The Last Lambs / 37

Fragment Of A Letter / 40

A Vietnam Veteran's Memorial Day / 43

Riding To Work / 44

Man On A Stick / 45

Dark Angel / 46

Charred / 47

51/49 / 48

Sudden Flight / 49

For Old Girl Friends / 50

Weights And Measures / 52

Working In The Yard / 53

Turning / 54

Elegy For White Birches / 56

Young Mothers In The Spring / 57

After The Rain / 59

Walking With Fireflies / 60

Migrating Birds / 61

About the poet / 62

CHILDREN OF THE DUST

In the mornings, barefoot they crouched,
two and three together, drawing circles in the dust,
their mothers calling out,
"Mouamar!"
"Manuel!"
"Yassir!"
"Augusto!"
Before masked men peered out car windows,
before the mosque crumbled stone by stone,
before a devil wind blistered their faces,
before little sister curled thin on her pallet,
they scratched symbols in the dust.

They squatted, playing games,
until one day, stained forever
on the pavement of their daydreams,
they looked up from the dust,
suddenly hardened like prehistoric fawn,
and heard the wails of their mothers,
"Mouamar!"
"Manuel!"
"Yassir!"
"Augusto!"
Before the commandante demanded too many pesos,
before they dragged father to the truck,
before the mudslide pushed the shanty down the hill,
before brother stepped in front of the bullet,
they danced together in the dust.

Now, they lean against the post office wall,

waiting for el capitan to switch the ignition.
They will sell you anything for hard currency.
They will defeat you any way they can.
They remember the outcries of their mothers,
"Mouamar!"
"Manuel!"
"Yassir!"
"Augusto!"
After the missle scattered concrete and glass,
after fever crawled into the village,
after their bellies became swollen and the flies bit,
after blood congealed on the cobblestones,
they whispered promises in the dust.

INITIATION

They lead Imamu through the streets.
The tribe with no father leads the boy
past the money changer, past the pawn shop,
past the liquor store, past graffiti.
They run Imamu through the streets.
Run, Joseph, run Joseph Imamu,
find the human sacrifice —
a man has been driven from his village.

They dress Imamu for the feast.
The tribe with no mother dresses the boy
in a chieftain's cap, in his ritual jacket,
in ceremonial shoes, in a dark fierce mask.
They chant Imamu a warrior's song.
Dance Joseph, dance Joseph Imamu,
grow cunning and surefooted —
women weep for the men they have lost.

They hand Imamu the long thin knife.
The tribe with no country hands the boy
a pistol with six bullets, a hand ax,
a baseball bat, a firebomb.
They arm Imamu for his first battle.
Hurry Joseph, hurry Joseph Imamu,
become quick and terrifying —
children cry for their ancestors.

Joseph Imamu, your moment has come.
The human sacrifice awaits you
at the bus stop by the drug store.
Capture him, Joseph, run him through —
call yourself boy no more.

LEATHER JACKETS

Only the janitor could open the transoms.
They locked the windows to stop us from running.
Our coaches carried four foot paddles
drilled with one inch holes,
slammed them into our asses
until our faces exploded,
swang again and again to break us in half.
A fourth of the freshman girls became mothers,
wailed loudly in the halls and blamed us.
Some of my friends did time or probation
for shoplifting, burglary, or car theft.
Others shot heroin in the bathrooms.
All of us escaped our homes for midnight asphalt,
swigging quart bottles of watery beer.
For gangs from other schools
we wound links of tire chain around fists
hidden in the pockets of our leather jackets,
hoping to sidestep an ice pick
or dodge a baseball bat.
From our parents and teachers we learned
to shield our faces with a raised elbow
and keep our best hand free.

AMERICAN DACHAU

If I had the power of Hitler's army, Kayla,
my tanks would rumble across the sunken asphalt
of your schoolyard prison,
and sweep you away to one of those neighborhoods
where sprinklers keep the bluegrass green
and little girls wear new
the dresses grandma brings from the thrift store rack.
I'd drive my tanks up the terraces of those pious men
who dole out pocket change and are fond of saying,
"God helps those who help themselves."
My tanks would circle your house, Kayla,
and you could sleep all night,
go to school without being afraid.
No one would stand you in line at the clinic.
No mean uncle would grind away your soul
against the rough ribs of a yellow mattress.

BALLS

Between geometry and philosophy
I learned about circles
going around forever.
I never understood about balls,
how they meant everything:
tropheys, courage, girls, money,
being counted in.
I never thought of balls
except for the trouble they caused me,
the smothering days in right field
where few came,
growling in commando enthusiasm
near the five yard line
through nights of ice.
My speciality was leaves —
their jagged edges,
their unlikely forms.

DISCOVERING THE SOLAR SYSTEM

He sat with them on a blanket
inhaling the moon through the pines.

Jim was there, Eddie
and Pamela with her bright face.

They knew what they believed
and he was strange, they said,
for not knowing.

When he told them he would never know,
except to feel a certain craving
looking up outside himself,
he lost Pamela
who insisted on knowing,
and Jim and Eddie
who swore they knew.

That was the night
he knew nothing and everything.

LION TAMERS

We old lion tamers
usually cry
at the damndest times:
reading the newspaper on the toilet,
watching TV while everyone sleeps.
An old lion tamer
can cry looking at the refrigerator.
We remember how it was.
We don't want any more paws.
Away loud growls and scary eyes,
away hurtful incisors,
once and for all.
We move around our houses
as we did our cages,
backs pressed against bars,
brandishing whips
in case they try to sneak in.
"Back, lion!" we snap.
"Back, beast!"
Even when we crack our whips
and shout commands,
we're still crying.
It's not easy being a retired lion tamer.
We remember all those times
we were six years old.

BUDDY

Begin with the face of a boy
vowing never to grow old.

With a rock, an arrowhead,
thrown sidearm curveball
across a vacant lot,
slash the first mark
between nose and cheek.

Add detail on a July night
with static lightning
and Johnny Walker Red.
Blow cigarette ash
into an aurora,
scar the forehead twice.

Distort it in a shower stall
at Fort Polk, Louisiana,
yell muddahfuckah,
punch it, stomp it.

Carve out the eyes
in the midnight rain
under the glare
of the buzzing sign
at the Helping Hand.

Glaze it over a grill
at a truck stop
on the interstate
with grease
from hamburgers, pork tenderloin,

eggs up and basted.

Mount it in the line
at the blood bank
on a side street downtown
9 a.m. to 4:30 p.m.,
Mondays and Thursdays,
on sale — $10 a pint.

ON PLATO

Really, what you are doing
is dreaming reality.
The dream smells foul,
keeps poking at you,
makes crying, moaning sounds.
Hunger is in it, and hurt.
It makes you eat reality.
It keeps stuffing reality down your throat
like sausage and swinebraten.
The tile feels cold through your socks.
The wish is to be someplace else.
The woman you want is someone else's.
You can imagine her naked,
i.e. her mythical forest.
What you need is money for Munich
but you don't have any.
The train station guard
shoves you away with a stick.
You want to invoke Plato,
tell the guard you're just a shadow,
you should ride for nothing,
but Plato's not available.
He's still beating the hell out of some idea
that's beating the hell out of you.
All you know about Plato is
he was a dog you had once.
Plato never stood on this spot.
He was never alone at the age of 19
on the streets of Frankfurt, Germany
at the end of the Twentieth Century.
You're certain he never felt

the urge to vomit this urgently.
He never lost his way
in a bathroom stall.
He never threw up
this much knowledge.

TWO YOUNG GAYS
WATCHING OLD MOVIES

Ballcaps flipped back,
they sit crosslegged
on the shag,
crunching tacos
off paper plates.

The flow of Garbo's ethereal scarves
across the black and white screen
transfixes them,
lures them into a baroque suite.

Outside
the Reverend Plague
clamps hairy knuckles and twisted chin
against the picture window,
locked out
until the final credits.

CHILDREN OF PAN

From birth they run
with instincts of wild ponies,
free of shoes and stockings,
dashing randomly through trees.

They too have been warned
of broken glass, gravel,
burrs, scorpions, yet
they scatter without warning,
galloping after an uncertain scent.

They cut heels, smash toes, anything
for the pleasure of bare skin
against grass, mud, tree bark,
rain puddle, cutting snow,
bound only by their urge
to scamper unshod and unshoed.

Neither reason nor fear
will deter these descendants
of satyrs and unicorns.

Reason turns them into stones;
fear into swans with no water.

THE PIGEONS OF CHERNOBLE

*(The day after the nuclear accident
at Chernoble, several hundred homing
pigeons competing in an annual race
were released in Lyons, France for a
destination in Brussels, Belgium. Unlike
previous races, only a few of the pigeons
arrived.)*

Each generation
fantasy birds visit earth.
Mozart knew them,
so did Freud.
For those who will listen
they tell stories
yet unwritten.
Revolutionaries shrill their slogans,
cannibals and cardinals
intone their forbidden canticles.
They dust sunsets with beatific visions.

Now they are scattered over Europe,
lost in a nuclear storm,
the cord to intuition
clipped in the wisp of a millisecond.
They sit dazed in the pine forests,
beaks ajar
like tiny children beaten for laughing.

An official inquiry has concluded:
"Many questions still abound."
I want to know
what exhortation they carried,
how they will go back,

whether their eyes have grown narrow or wide,
if they feel as I did,
a boy falling backward
off a porch into a spreader bush,
hearing the laughter of aunts and uncles,
my mother saying, "You'll be all right."

Already I had entered
the unremitting dark.

SNAPPING BEANS, 1955

Four brothers and a sister
squat on overturned buckets
around a basement drain
snapping beans, listening to a woman
with a sunshine voice
sing a song on the radio
about falling in love.

Behind them
mason jars sit in the musk
of homemade pine shelves,
dented pots on an antique stove
bubble with tomatoes and rhubarb.
Sauerkraut fermenting
in a chipped crock from Austria
mixes a sweet sour scent
with mold in the stone walls.

This tableau has been staged in memory.
It doesn't tell how they fought,
how deals were made:
you scrub them down,
you snap the tips,
you break them into equal parts.

It doesn't tell
what they sealed inside,
why the youngest boy, even now,
crimps his mouth
to hide oversized teeth,

why the girl poses sideways,
fearing laughter and her image
on the other side of the lens.

It doesn't tell
they crouched like that
all afternoon in July heat,
forced into a circle
they would never comprehend,
scooping handfuls of wet beans
from chipped porcelain tubs,
snapping segments
of snicker and shadow,
dividing time so fast
they never noticed
their wrinkled hands.

HORNETS

They simmered up the window panes
inside my uncle's farmhouse,
their black pointed tails curling
against sun stained curtain lace
in the bedroom where we had been jailed
for an afternoon nap.
In those summers before the family scattered
into suburban cul-de-sacs and air-conditioned bungalows,
we believed their fearsome power
had been summoned to hold us there.
We heard our mothers shuffle pots
on a wood stove, slam pie plates into the oven,
rattle silver and dishes for the evening meal.
Through the window I saw a real bluebird
hang over the brown, rutted barnyard and disappear
behind jalopies half sunken on bone naked axles,
gouged windshields and amputated doors.
Cousins and brothers, we sweltered
in the musk of stale wallpaper paste,
then broke with the past, slid
off the cast iron bed, howled
as they stung our naked feet,
their wings slapping the wooden floor.
Even now at reunions, we hold the tender skin
of our arches up to the light,
marvel at the terror branded
in those thin white scars.

DRY RIVER

Our country uncle
has an old hunter's tricky eyes.
He leads us
under a rotting log bridge
into the riverbed
to spot rabbits
hidden behind
dangling tree roots.

I breath the air
in the channel's flow,
my lungs calm and controlled
as the rabbits we have come to kill.

Our boots crunch stones and mulch
as we step the river's course.
Beyond the second curve
we file up a ravine
that rises and lopes through cottonwoods
onto the prairie.

Just before I reach the ridge
the memory of another river
holds me back,
its name and place and time unrecorded
except for my silt blown eyes and whirling hair,
my body tumbling its murky passage,
me waking wet in the dark
from that nightmare of my own drowning.

COTTONMOUTHS

My father has never seen so many.
They warm themselves on a boulder
one hundred feet below
on the coal pit's rim,
rearing square oversized jaws,
writhing into knots and untangling.
They drop into the water one by one,
push rabid foamy pods
across the scorched surface
with trap sprung mouths,
mount the boulder again.
We sit above them, tackle box at our feet,
our eyes held by their fangs
until sun burns the morning clear.
There will be another time to fish.

WESTERN KANSAS GIRL

Her mind opens through the windshield
over a straight highway,
eyes squaring the fields neatly
left and right.

She marks her progress
with grain elevators and population signs
every twenty miles or so.

Don't confuse her
with mountains or skyscrapers
or wide rivers.
She wants creeks and stone fences,
abandoned silos and windmills,
cows huddled on a sagebrush slope.

Dry spidery forms
tumble in her dreams,
cottonwoods shimmer,
sunsets draw her west.

Now and then
she stops at a crossing
to watch the evening train
bolting to New Mexico.

BUFFALO MOUNTAIN

Stone dark snow atop a distant peak
strikes cold within.
It reaches relentlessly downhill,
spreading a vastness
no one controls or understands.
Safe behind a windowpane
I still feel what once clung together
crumbling wall by wall
in the tiny rooms of the heart.

TEQUA CREEK

We see our faces, two of us,
propped on our hands,
images changing in the current,
a breeze stroking the ravine.
Above us, our car, parked in a hurry,
slants off the black highway.

The farmer rolling his tractor across the bridge
glances down and might surmise
city people are fishing or digging arrowheads,
not trying to divine our own narcissus
or compare what we say with what we are.

For me, its course muddies sacred
in the afternoon glow, a relic, centuries old,
the bridge an afterthought.
For her, it is enough they lived here,
Shawnee Indians, they and their children,
faces turned toward the sun,
watching hawk and owl and the circling of clouds.

The water shows us nothing
but smooth stones.

A LION IN KANSAS

*(Based on sightings reported
in the Kansas City Star)*

The latch didn't click.
Grackles, feeding nearby, looked up.
Treefrogs in the hedgerow
halted evensong, then churned
their hysterical chant to higher decibels.
The lion nuzzled the gate and stepped out,
so emblazoned, it shivered at itself.

Newspapers report
rumors of the escape,
five, ten years apart,
but few will believe a lion
walked away through a ripe wheat field
while the world slept like a circus drunk.

They will say another kind of beast
subtracts their herds
one calf at a time,
slides down furrows, circles barns and silos,
parts the corn with its own colors.

Not many find an unlocked door
or startle certainty with a silhouette.
Some have seen a lion
walking in Kansas,
have gone to quiet their horses
in the glare of the moon
and found its print
deep in the crusted snow.

HORSE ON A HILL

Along this strip of new highway
miles of pasture
rise and fall without farmhouse or barn.
At the top of one straw cut ridge
a stallion kisses the ground.
Wind sculpts his mane,
a monument,
reddish brown against sky.
He rears and opens his throat
to the horizon.
My car will be one of many.

THE YOUNG HUSBAND

Even if she says, "Don't go, I had a dream,"
you must go.
She will beg to go with you
but you must go alone.
You must not promise to return
because you may not.
You must go and find that place and be there.
It may be a day, or a year, or many years.

You must set out
not knowing where your feet will lead.
You might sleep under a certain tree
or go down into a cave with no light.
You might walk beside bear or elk
or fly a whole season near the sun.
You might build a dam across a stream
or float in a clear pool,
reflecting only light and shade.
You must go to that place,
see what must be seen,
do what must be done.

If you return
she will know you by your face
but your shoulders will be as broad
as the tree you slept under,
your eyes deep
as that cave.

THE FARMER'S WIDOW AT HIS GRAVE

Rest now and let your knuckles grow smooth.
Hammer no clouds against the sky.
On this hillside, conjure no more grain.
Let fences and sheds fall down.
Let combines rust.
Let all things be as they will be.
Let our youthful design complete itself
as the landscape subscribes,
by sun, vermin and the wind's fury.
No longer will I come into this field
with food and drink and a lover's kiss.
No longer will we bloody our hands
at the cry of a newborn calf.
No longer will we sleep with the sunset
or dress together before first light.
Forget these things and the sayings of men.
They explain nothing
of the formations of your face,
tilled by seasons of infidelities,
nothing of your stooped shape, your hands
busted and scabbed by frozen mornings,
nothing of the hues of the afternoons
that stretched our shadows
beyond all reckoning.

THE LAST LAMBS

That was when
the young priest
opened the parish gym
on week nights
to keep us off the streets,
cornered us one by one
demanding to know how many times
since our last confession
we spilled our holy seed,
promised us paradise
if we kept our fists
out of our pants.

And when
girls like Rosemary
from the convent school
poked against us
in the wild, windy midnights,
their mothers in ragged gowns
hissing through cracks
in screen doors,
girls like Rosemary
who panted until their skin shook,
then stepped back
because the good sisters implored them
not to step down,
sent us home feverish
to wait for something better.

And when
police stalked us

through glaring, dangerous streets
because we happened to be there,
mexican, black,
youngest in a family of ten.
We searched alleys and trash bins
looking for booze or fistfights,
something to steal or break,
running from the young priest
who wanted us to wrestle or box
or play basketball,
tell him how many times that week
we hungered for girls like Rosemary
with scented hair and the warm place
we could feel through their skirts.

When the red eyes of patrol cars
turned a corner suddenly,
we hid under old chevys,
ripped our shirts and our skin
rolling over fences
to escape being slammed
against paddy wagons,
to escape being beaten into better boys,
willing and ready to sacrifice.

And when
the ex football player, the ex marine,
the newborn Christian
campaigning for city council,
came to our school
to tell us of the vision he had for our future
and explain how he once felt as we did,
felt he knew everything

but now he knew better,
knew we could create a better world
and be like our forefathers,
the founders of the Republic,
the great generals, the great frontiersmen,
who believed in God, hard work and gold,
if we'd only listen and obey
and sacrifice.

And just beyond those days
we woke one morning
to see the dream of our future
brighten under a banner headline
in the photograph of the rumpled carcass
of a helicopter gunship
smoking human flesh
in a place we never heard of
along the muddy road to Hue.

FRAGMENT OF A LETTER

Tommy, all the short timers say
they'll write when they get home.
They never do, they
disappear into a future
we'll never see
with a girl we'll never know.
The face of the girl
who keeps coming to us
in dreams
fades quickly in morning confusion,
makes us sick with envy
wondering who she's loving now.

I won't be like the others, Tommy,
I won't forget to write.
I'm going to write you
every time I'm back over there,
on days I can't think straight,
days like today in this autumn light
so red and so orange
I think the trees are crying.

In this red autumn
they're burning fires
making the air hazy and distant
like a day on the rubber plantation.
The smoke burns fresh,
the aroma of a newly lit cigarette
in a wet pine grove.

When I start laughing to myself
no one sees what's so funny.
They don't know it's you I'm laughing about,
you who could always make me laugh.
You could hardly move your mouth,
and you said, "Now look at my fucking face.
Now I'll never have a girlfriend."
None of us could stop laughing,
not even the medics lifting you
into the chopper as fast as they could.

Back here everybody's laughing
in a different kind of world.
I don't know what to say,
who to tell it to
or how to make sense.
I move with the crowds,
don't recognize any faces,
don't know the words to their songs.

I watch the news,
waiting for you to reappear
in backpack and fatigues,
waiting to hear you speak again.
And I don't know where you are
or how to mail a letter
to a dream of a war
I was in a long time ago.
That's all you are, Tommy,

a dream, just another beatup
dragged down fucked up dream
I had one humid year
when I was too young to know better.

Don't get the idea
I forgot to write,
because I will finish this letter
one day soon
and put it in the mail.

A VIETNAM VETERAN'S MEMORIAL DAY

We weep today for those
whose names are carved on this wall,
for those whose bodies
tumble in distant waters,
for those who've never returned
from the dust of another country.

We weep too for these old soldiers
standing here to the boom of the guns
and the haunted brass of bitter bugles.
They empty their tears for themselves,
for the lies they believed,
for the boys they once were
before they learned to kill.

RIDING TO WORK

The gods of morning call to us
when we retrieve the news
outside the wrought iron door.
They speak through birds and leaves
and the silence that falls down cool.

Old Ed Bean arrives in his dented coup,
arguing politics and baseball.
A great leaping beast laps at the tailpipe,
redfaced, disjointed, frisky,
its tongue long and raw as sunrise.

We join other cars on the freeway,
take turns saying, "Once this was a farm."
The creature chases us as far as the bridge,
falls behind, and the city
collects its toll.

In the compound of brick and traffic lights
faces in car windows become clear.
We congregate in office malls
for soup and salad and bring home music
to wail by in the evening.

In leather recliners we'll sink
in television light,
flipping for plots with surprise endings,
calamity in Peru,
somebody's love affair.

MAN ON A STICK

Across the street the shades of his English Tudor
kept us out, kept out the moving van and
two young marrieds with a baby.
Our white sneakers flashed at butterfly pace
as we unloaded a contemporary chair.
Each day something new arrived:
drapes, a refrigerator, the fireplace screen.
Nurserymen followed, tearing out
the brown and twisted fibers of old garden beds.
A fence company pulled down yards of chain link
and squared the lawn with pointed wrought iron.
Looking out bay windows we could see his nurse
lead him step by step down the brick walk
to a place under the canopy of oaks
where he stood with a rumpled hat,
leaning on a tall, carved cane,
looking up from below his shoulders
like a turtle in cool grass.
Above him, each leaf opened and closed in turn,
clattering against each other.
At first we waved at our new neighbor,
and shouted, "Hello, Mr. Miller,"
but he kept his silence and his back to us.
Ours was a budding life.

DARK ANGEL

A man in a white pickup truck
tries to run me down
in a covered parking lot.
Seeing me caught
between cement ceiling
and asphalt floor,
he rages around a row of cars
zigzagging blue rubber smoke,
and closing the distance,
aims the grill
at my heart.
When I jump aside
I see his eyes,
his aura glowing through the windshield.
He jerks the truck away
through the shadowy columns,
leaving me light headed
in the exhaust.
One day another spirit
will try to lock my image
in his hell bent gaze.
To claim me,
he must swerve left
one more inch.

CHARRED

I'd been thinking all night about god,
thinking there was nothing to think.

From that balcony overlooking the trees
I could see nothing beyond galaxies,
nothing more than a few clouds
just outside the spheres of my eyes.

A breeze fanned their tarot shapes
across the August sky.

It was that one cloud,
a dark and cloven cloud
between me and the moon,
that sent me inside, locking all doors,
sent me curling under the sheets
deeper into my center
like burning parchment
to blasphemous truth.

51/49

Here's how
we'll break our standoff:
You call the shots,
elect your own board of directors,
write a book and be famous,
tell me how it should be done.
Just give me a pair of shorts
and, oh, about fifty bucks.
Give me a few good years
with a girl named Karla,
a French/Indian/Spanish/worldwise girl
living in the Caribbean.
Remember, life's just numbers:
I'll get her and trade you
my lousy little point.
Think of it,
a penny's worth of paradise
for maximum control,
all the myocardial infarctions
you can handle,
all the CVA's
you can steal.
I'll still own
my own ass
100%.

SUDDEN FLIGHT

The rabbi says,
"His death tells us:
Beware the jolt,
the trap door.
Beware the moment
no one knows
until it comes."

Leaves churn in the heat.
Women beat their breasts and wail.
He is not the man in the eulogy.
His life never knew that much joy.
His family never loved him well.

When the kaddish begins
a hidden jay
flashes over the burial tent,
squawks three times three
and joins the blue haze.

FOR OLD GIRL FRIENDS

A man never suffers the depths of his own cruelty
until his daughter recognizes him for the first time.
He cradles the nascent woman and beholds her eyes.
The human in her fixes his image and trusts him.
He lifts her to his face and inhales her,
a breeze that's settled in his lap.
He turns his ear to her voice and sings
though he can't remember when last he sung.
He smooths his palm across her head
and shudders at how breakable it must be.
Her own hands cannot be reproduced by any form of art.

Over time, she begins to skip ahead of him through the grass,
hums for no special reason. He marvels at her exhuberance,
laughs when her arguments outdistance his. He discovers
a quality he lacks but has no definition for. Her ways
terrify him, he fears something unknown will crush her
and she will vanish with the best of his memories. She
grows taller, bolder, more private. He watches her
test herself in the mirror, pleading for approval,
notices how much time it takes and how carefully
she draws herself new with pencil and brush,
how often she pulls a comb through her hair.

When the doorbells rings, he smiles with her,
her face anticipating the boy outside.

Late in the night, when her sobs shake the settled house,
he carries her pain with him outside and sits alone,
feeling each sob again as he confesses the Spring Dance when
he stood up the girl who had already bought his boutonniere;

the woman dressed for dinner he told he could never love.
He confesses the lies he authored, his battering wit,
his need to feel victorious and draw tears.
He confesses these and other unthinkable sorrows
to the old breezes haunting him now, to the faces
of the women who took him in with their eyes
and trusted him to see them human. He hates himself,
hates his whining voice begging to give them back
what he stripped away.

WEIGHTS AND MEASURES

The walnut table stands between us
a distance of thirty years.
On it we weigh our jaws against our fists,
measure the diameter of our breathing,
the circumference of our love and hate.
We feel the volume of our emptiness
in proportion to the volume of our voices.
The tonnage of old words holds down our tongues
until we hear our voices splinter and crack:
you are not my father, I told you once;
you are no son of mine, you shouted back.
Only when we push the table aside,
thirty years after it pulled us apart,
only then, all distance, all weight, all volume,
becomes compressed between the chests
of two sobbing men who measured
each motion, each word,
too often, too long.

WORKING IN THE YARD

The older couple on the corner
scratches the ground with antique rakes
day after day after the last snow melts.
They complain that leaves blown from other yards
clutter the chiseled terraces
of their newly mowed lawn.

Wrapped in sweaters and stocking hats,
these yard people bag up winter's bones,
clip, chop and haul,
even as weeds begin to blossom.
A month ago they trimmed the spreader bushes
whose huge, cool shadows now darken the marigolds.

Squirrels attack the feeder they have hung
for the redbird, thrush and titmouse.
"A blamed squirrel can eat anything,"
they keep saying over the fence,
and contrive baffles and screen guards
to keep the tree rats out.
They spend the day spraying the spruces
spider mites are sucking dry.

When the Angelus tolls,
man, woman and a squirrel,
who slouches behind them unseen,
squint together in the advancing dusk,
fold their hands on their bellies.

TURNING

You ate cherries in brandy
and couldn't stop laughing.
The regulars at the bar,
the old waiter carrying schnapps,
the violinist stroking Vivaldi,
the gods in the fountain,
everyone and everything
seemed soft,
brushed with a shimmering
from the tops of trees,
gesturing slow motion:
leaves to the sun.

Then sunlight sped.
Shadows on the cobblestones
drew a hypotenuse.
One couple left, and two more.
I craved another gin,
but they folded the umbrellas
and you looked away,
smoothing your hair
under the brim of an oval hat.
"It's getting cold," I said,
for nothing else to say.

I must have seen you again
but I don't remember anything you said,
just your postcard
from somewhere in Spain
reminding me how we left the cafe
through the wrought iron gate,

stood hand in hand on the corner.
We didn't want to leave,
me to my office,
you to your house,
to your husband.
We wanted to stand there forever
in the happy confusion
of an October afternoon.

The driver of a hansom
waved at us with a folded whip,
cracked it near the horse's shoulder
and rumbled past,
the spoked wheels turning,
turning fast.

ELEGY FOR WHITE BIRCHES

(Destroyed by Drought
and Borers)

Your rustle sounded of light feathers
migrating into night.

At dawn I watched you skimming grass,
a white stroke
sketched upward out of green,
breeze lifted
by slender drooping branches.

Your leaves shimmered at high noon.

What you lacked was pond, marsh,
the brotherhood of reeds.
Hatched here on this dry infested plain
you sought dark moving water,
found searing sky.

In cool shadows
the fine parchment of your heron limbs
rose into dusk.

YOUNG MOTHERS IN THE SPRING

Was my mother ever as beautiful
as these women in fresh clothes,
waiting for their men to come home?

They move unhurried across Friday afternoon lawns
with sandaled children dangling
off slender white fingers
and a babe
held one handed between their breasts.

They've brushed back their hair
and though their lips aren't painted pink,
they only need the shadows of trees
to accent their unlined faces
against the solid color of grass.

They wear their opened blouses
outside shorts cut off mid thigh,
or floral dresses sliding easy in the wind
down naked shoulders to a V.
They can shift the newborn to one side
and stoop to pull a weed
all in one smooth motion.

I think they bathed the infant first
and then the curly haired boy
and then themselves,
and their mouths must taste
as sweet as lilac.

Once the car turns into the drive
they'll sit together on the deck

while he lights the coals
and tells about the passing of the day,
about grandma: they think she's dying.

This is the way it was supposed to be,
the way I dreamed it.
The oldest plays between us
on redwood slats,
and we laugh at what he shouldn't ask.

With this kind of breeze
and the leaves spawning early this year,
we move inside to lay the baby down
and sing the boy to sleep.
We kiss just like before
in a room open to the night.

I know about such a room.
I had a spring like this
with a young woman in fresh clothes,
her breasts full and high,
a whole summer
straining upward to the universe.

But my husbandry has long been lost
to wayward shrubs and sudden storms.
I must drive on now
to landscapes assigned to older men.

AFTER THE RAIN

I resist the urge to walk,
tell myself: sit and listen.

Sunlight returns shade by shade.
The green glows so brightly
my eyes close.

Bird sounds enter the stillness.

Insects resume mating calls.

Water splashes everywhere,
falls sphere by sphere,
from branch to leaf,
in uneven percussion.

Wind presses slowly
through the center of things.

Something inside blossoms:
not message, not messenger,
a wordless bloom.

WALKING WITH FIREFLIES

Dusk blues the rain damp hills.
Trees lean into the landscape,
their shadows tumbling
into dark.

The June you feared
blossoms into uncertainty,
into a June of no answers,
early cicadas, the late mayfly
facing you through the glass.

This is the June of aimless walking,
the trumpeting of the crow,
fluting frogs,
bats stirring the sunset yolk.
This is the June of walking with fireflies
when the incandescence of the heart
finally burns.

You stride across sour grass
flickering lost details
at the orange edges of memory,
illuminate for yourself
with each blink of the eye
what you were then, what you are now.

MIGRATING BIRDS

Autumn comes
in quiet discourse
to spirits departing.
What once glowed and soared
slows and holds
in the aggregation
of specks so distant
they can only be imagined
for the things they are.
We below
remain with what we've wrought:
lies told,
lucky pennies spent,
peonies trimmed to mud.
In the absence
of honeysuckle and thunderhead,
in the chill that precedes
the whisper of snow
and finality of ice,
the unspoken can be seen now
up high,
clear.

Bill Bauer lives and writes in Summit County, Colorado and on the Caribbean island of Sint Maarten. Prior to the sale of his company in 1992, he was a cofounder and the president of Media/Professional Insurance, Inc., a firm that specializes in defending the First Amendment rights of the media. He graduated with a degree in English Literature from Rockhurst College in 1965 and worked as a reporter for the *Kansas City Star*. His National Guard Unit was activated during the race riots of 1968 and he was sent to Vietnam the following year. A native of Kansas City, Missouri he is married and the father of two children.

His first book of poetry, *The Eye Of The Ghost*, won the 1985 BkMk Press Missouri Poet's Award.

OTHER Bk Mk OFFERINGS

Moving the Seasons, thirty-eight poems and nine reformations by Charles Guenther. "I have much to learn from [his] enviable skills and long devotions." —*Howard Nemerov;* "I love French poetry and there's no better translator of it than Charles Guenther. So many masterpieces of the art. . . . A book to reread again and again."—*Charles Simic.*

$12.00, 80 pages, paper

Forever Is Easy, poems by Lynne Burris Butler. "When I read Lynne Butler's work I feel good about the state of lyric poetry in the land and the place of both love and common sense in the line."—*Miller Williams;* "Witty, American to the bone, Lynne Butler has a wicked eye for the outrageous and uproarious . . ."—*Colette Inez.*

$9.00, 64 pages, paper

Stations of the Air, poems by John Ciardi; selected by Miller Williams. Thirty-three never before published poems by a true master of poetics and poetry translation. A last breath of genius from one of the great literary men of our time. This offering will continue to enrich the lives of alert readers who care about the depth of engagement and subtlety of interpretation. Illustrated with a full color surrealist painting by Michael Bergt.

$10.50, 64 pages, cloth w/jacket

Starting a Swan Dive, poems by Patricia Cleary Miller. "Many of the women in these poems need the experience of being desired so keenly they have accepted the risk-taking involved. The extremity of fulfillment is to be found on the brink of danger."—*Hilda Morley;* "Patricia Cleary Miller's poems toss and turn like lovers seeking ecstasy."—*Gloria Vando Hickok.*

$9.00, 64 pages, paper

Other People's Lives, poems by Catherine N. Parke. "There is no short cut to this kind of poetry. The power of its ideas and the delicacy of its verbal effects lift it high above the level of most of what is being written in our time—most, indeed, of what has been written at any time."—*John Wain;* "Catherine Parke's poems are agile and sardonic, meditative and lyrical, always engrossing . . ."—*Sandra M. Gilbert.*

$9.00, 64 pages, paper

Hard Freeze, poems by Philip Miller. "These poems are about impasse, stasis and silence. Hard to imagine more difficult subjects, which is exactly what makes this collection so extraordinary. Philip Miller speaks about a frozen passage . . . to a reconstitution of self."—*Neal Bowers;* "Miller's poems are marked by an intimate, easy quality. Many flow like chiffon; others are as dense as grief. Some dream with startling endings."—*Alice Brand.*

$9.00, 64 pages, paper